POEMS *to* LIVE BY

In Uncertain Times

POEMS

to

LIVE BY

In Uncertain Times

EDITED BY *Joan Murray*

BEACON PRESS
BOSTON

Beacon Press
25 Beacon Street
Boston, Massachusetts 02108-2892
www.beacon.org

Beacon Press books
are published under the auspices of
the Unitarian Universalist Association of Congregations.

09 08 07 06 05   13 12 11 10 9

This book is printed on acid-free paper that meets the uncoated paper
ANSI/NISO specifications for permanence as revised in 1992.

Text design and composition by Melissa Ehn at
Wilsted & Taylor Publishing Services

Library of Congress Control Number: 2001097289

We glimpsed them through the rubble:
the ones who lost their lives,
the heroes' double burials,
the ones now "left behind."

CONTENTS

IV. We Are Running
Warnings and Instructions

V. End and Beginning
War and Rumors of War

VI.   Little Prayers
Meditations and Conversations

INTRODUCTION

It's been more than sixty years since Kenneth Burke spoke of literature as equipment for living. In my life, I've found this to be true. Difficult events—whether personal or historic—have a way of overwhelming us; they can leave us weeping, raging, or numb. All the words of politicians, experts, and reporters only add to the muddle and our sense of powerlessness. But poems can cut through confusion to speak knowingly and intimately to us and stir us from within.

Knowing this, I've kept an eye open for poems that help me through such times, because they move me or caution me, buck me up or lighten me up. I was lucky to find Lucille Clifton's "we are running" when I was rushing off to a job that would have proved disastrous to me as a poet. Robert Bly's "Things to Think" arrived when I was overburdened by obligations yet certain that the world would fall apart without me. I keep both of those poems, along with many others by poets of our era, in a binder labeled "Poems to Live By."

They do me good. They do others good (so my friends tell me). They're better than a flashlight in the dark.

I hadn't planned on gathering them into a book—until the attack on the World Trade Center persuaded me to do so. It left me, like most people, overwhelmed by a tremendous sense of loss. A few days later, in the café car of a train, I met six young firemen on their way to New York to dig at the wreckage site. They were nervous—and excited. We all knew it was unlikely that survivors would be found, and silently we understood what their task would be. Yet by coming forward to do this very difficult thing, they had stepped across some line and had become larger than themselves. They seemed to be lit from within.

I realized they were people my parents' generation would have recognized—the sort of people who'd been missing from "the scene." Yet now, with all the footage of the victims, survivors, and rescue workers, people like them—who went about their lives, did their jobs, and cared deeply about one another and this nation—were suddenly visible again.

I went back to my seat and began a poem, "Survivors—Found." It shot out of me, in ballad form, like someone spontaneously leaping up to sing. Emerson would have said the poem was hovering out there, and it was my task to pull it down. It was clearly an occasional poem, admittedly not a great poem. But it had the force of an inevitable poem, as if someone needed it.

Someone needed to see that despite the loss of thousands of brave, generous, everyday people, many more like them had been found—right next door.

Four days after I wrote it, I read "Survivors—Found" on National Public Radio's *Morning Edition*. At once, phone calls, letters, and messages began pouring in. Thousands of strangers were contacting me to thank me, or they were hitting the NPR website or the website of the writers institute where I work. Most wanted copies so they could read it to others —at a factory in Michigan, a police department in Maryland, a doctors' conference in Canada. E-mail messages came from Indonesia, Israel, and Italy. One woman phoned from her office in North Carolina because her mother didn't understand one of the lines.

I was moved by these people's urgent and unembarrassed need for a poem—for words that cut through all the pages and pages of reportage (so they told me) and addressed their anxiety and deep sense of loss. I knew that they (as well as I) had a need for other poems—*truly* great poems—poems from many other voices and viewpoints. So I got my binder, and I added other poems to it.

Which poems were needed in this uncertain time (or *any* of our uncertain times)? Poems that deal with loss and remembrance—to let us grieve and begin to heal. Poems about dark times to make us see we're not the only ones to face them. Poems that offer hope now —and prepare us to return to joy. Poems to remind us of our responsibilities to others in this world. Poems to help us see war from experienced perspectives. And poems to let us pray—even if we find it hard to believe.

Someone else might make different choices, but these are the sixty poems I find most useful now. Maybe you'll find some of them useful too. (Either now or later.) If you do, why not copy them down by hand—so they become part of you—and put them in a binder. Then go to a bookstore and pick up a couple of books by the poets who wrote them. Now you've got some real equipment for living.

Joan Murray

Survivors—Found

 JOAN MURRAY

*W*e thought that they were gone—
we rarely saw them on our screens—
those everyday Americans
with workaday routines,

and the heroes standing ready—
not glamorous enough—
on days without a tragedy,
we clicked—and turned them off.

We only saw the cynics—
the dropouts, show-offs, snobs—
the right- and left-wing critics:
we saw that they were us.

But with the wounds of Tuesday
when the smoke began to clear,
we rubbed away our stony gaze—
and watched them reappear:

the waitress in the tower,
the broker reading mail,
the pair of window washers
filling up a final pail,

the husband's last "I love you"
from the last seat of a plane,
the tourist taking in a view
no one would see again,

the fireman, his eyes ablaze
as he climbed the swaying stairs—
he knew someone might still be saved.
We wondered *who* it was.

We glimpsed them through the rubble:
the ones who lost their lives,
the heroes' *double* burials,
the ones now "left behind,"

the ones who rolled *a* sleeve up,
the ones in scrubs and masks,
the ones who lifted buckets
filled with stone and grief and ash:

some spoke a different language—
still no one missed a phrase;
the soot had softened every face
of every shade and age—

"the greatest generation"?—
we wondered where they'd gone—
they hadn't left directions
how to find our nation-home:

for thirty years we saw few signs,
but now in swirls of dust,
they were alive—they had survived—
we saw that they were us.

I

I THINK
CONTINUALLY
of THOSE

Death and Remembrance

When Autumn Came

 Faiz Ahmed Faiz

Translated by Naomi Lazard

This is the way that autumn came to the trees:
it stripped them down to the skin,
            left their ebony bodies naked.
It shook out the yellow leaves which were their
    hearts,
scattered them over the ground.
Whoever wanted to trampled them out of shape;
not a single moan of protest was heard.

Birds that herald dreams
became strangers to their voice
when their song was throttled.
            They dropped into the dust
even before the hunter strung his bow.

Oh, God of May, have mercy.
Bless these withered bodies

with the passion of your resurrection,
make their dead veins flow with blood.

Give some tree the gift of green again.
Let one bird sing.

What you knew of me

 EUGENIO MONTALE

Translated by Jonathan Galassi

*W*hat you knew of me
was only a coat of paint,
the veil that clothes
our human fate.

And maybe behind the canvas
was the still blue;
only a seal kept out
the limpid sky.

Or else it was the fiery
change in me,
revealing a burning ember
I'll never see.

So that this husk became
my true substance;

the fire that isn't quenched
for me was called: ignorance.

If you see a shadow
it's no shadow—it's me.
If only I could tear it off
and offer it to you.

Sleeping in the Forest

 MARY OLIVER

I thought the earth
remembered me, she
took me back so tenderly, arranging
her dark skirts, her pockets
full of lichens and seeds. I slept
as never before, a stone
on the riverbed, nothing
between me and the white fire of the stars
but my thoughts, and they floated
light as moths among the branches
of the perfect trees. All night
I heard the small kingdoms breathing
around me, the insects, and the birds
who do their work in the darkness. All night
I rose and fell, as if in water, grappling
with a luminous doom. By morning
I had vanished at least a dozen times
into something better.

Otherwise

 JANE KENYON

I got out of bed
on two strong legs.
It might have been
otherwise. I ate
cereal, sweet
milk, ripe, flawless
peach. It might
have been otherwise.
I took the dog uphill
to the birch wood.
All morning I did
the work I love.

At noon I lay down
with my mate. It might
have been otherwise.
We ate dinner together
at a table with silver
candlesticks. It might

have been otherwise.
I slept in a bed
in a room with paintings
on the walls, and
planned another day
just like this day.
But one day, I know,
it will be otherwise.

Lake Song

 COLETTE INEZ

*E*very day our name is changed,
say stones colliding into waves.
Go read our names on the shore,
say waves colliding into stones.

Birds over water call their names
to each other again and again
to say where they are.
Where have you been, my small bird?

I know our names will change one day
to stones in a field
of anemones and lavender.

Before you read the farthest wave,
before our shadows disappear
in a starry blur, call out your name
to say where we are.

Mentioning of Souls

 GERALD STERN

If I get up one more time in the dark
you will have to cover me up completely
I will be shaking so much from the cold.
And if my voice trembles as I go from room
     to room
you will have to leave your own luxury
to see if I am just moaning or already talking
     to the dead.
If you come into the kitchen
you will see how painful it is
to cross over to the dark stove;
if you sit with me one whole night
you will see how slow the hours go
in front of the hanging plants.
Stand by the crowded window for five minutes
and watch the light come in through the
     crippled birch.
You can laugh a little

at my wolfish soul staring at the moon;
you can close your eyes
as I say the names,
and remember, with your own lips,
as I go over the victories and the failures.

Time Does Not Bring Relief

 EDNA ST. VINCENT MILLAY

Time does not bring relief; you all have lied
Who told me time would ease me of my pain!
I miss him in the weeping of the rain;
I want him at the shrinking of the tide;
The old snows melt from every mountainside,
And last year's leaves are smoke in every lane;
But last year's bitter loving must remain
Heaped on my heart, and my old thoughts abide.
There are a hundred places where I fear
To go—so with his memory they brim.
And entering with relief some quiet place
Where never fell his foot or shone his face
I say, "There is no memory of him here!"
And so stand stricken, so remembering him.

I Think Continually of Those

 STEPHEN SPENDER

I think continually of those who were truly great.
Who, from the womb, remembered the soul's history
Through corridors of light where the hours are suns,
Endless and singing. Whose lovely ambition
Was that their lips, still touched with fire,
Should tell of the spirit clothed from head to foot in song.
And who hoarded from the spring branches
The desires falling across their bodies like blossoms.

What is precious is never to forget
The delight of the blood drawn from ageless springs
Breaking through rocks in worlds before our earth;
Never to deny its pleasure in the simple morning light.
Nor its grave evening demand for love;
Never to allow gradually the traffic to smother
With noise and fog the flowering of the spirit.

Near the snow, near the sun, in the highest fields
See how these names are fêted by the waving grass,

And by the streamers of white cloud,
And whispers of wind in the listening sky;
The names of those who in their lives fought for life,
Who wore at their hearts the fire's center.
Born of the sun they traveled a short while towards
    the sun,
And left the vivid air signed with their honor.

My child blossoms sadly

YEHUDA AMICHAI

Translated by Ruth Nevo

My child blossoms sadly.
He blossoms in spring without me,
he ripens in the sadness of my not being there.
I saw a cat playing with her kittens.
I shall not teach my son war,
I shall not teach him at all. I shall not be.
He puts sand in a small bucket.
He makes a sand cake.
I put sand in my body.
The cake crumbles. My body.

You Finish It: I Can't

 DANIEL BERRIGAN

*T*he world is somewhere visibly round,
perfectly lighted, firm, free in space,

but why men die like kings or
sick animals, why tears stand
in living faces, why one forgets

the color of the eyes of the dead—

II

IN A DARK TIME

Fear and Suffering

September

 JENNIFER MICHAEL HECHT

Tonight there must be people who are getting what
    they want.
I let my oars fall into the water.
Good for them. Good for them, getting what they want.

The night is so still that I forget to breathe.
The dark air is getting colder. Birds are leaving.

Tonight there are people getting just what they need.

The air is so still that it seems to stop my heart.
I remember you in a black and white photograph
taken this time of some year. You were leaning against
a half-shed tree, standing in the leaves the tree had lost.

When I finally exhale it takes forever to be over.

Tonight, there are people who are so happy,
that they have forgotten to worry about tomorrow.

Somewhere, people have entirely forgotten about
tomorrow.
My hand trails in the water.
I should not have dropped those oars. Such a
soft wind.

In a Dark Time

 THEODORE ROETHKE

*I*n a dark time, the eye begins to see,
I meet my shadow in the deepening shade;
I hear my echo in the echoing wood—
A lord of nature weeping to a tree.
I live between the heron and the wren,
Beasts of the hill and serpents of the den.

What's madness but nobility of soul
At odds with circumstances? The day's on fire!
I know the purity of pure despair,
My shadow pinned against a sweating wall.
That place among the rocks—is it a cave,
Or winding path? The edge is what I have.

A steady storm of correspondences!
A night flowing with birds, a ragged moon,
And in broad day the midnight come again!
A man goes far to find out what he is—
Death of the self in a long, tearless night,
All natural shapes blazing unnatural light.

Dark, dark my light, and darker my desire.
My soul, like some heat-maddened summer fly,
Keeps buzzing at the sill. Which I is *I*?
A fallen man, I climb out of my fear.
The mind enters itself, and God the mind,
And one is One, free in the tearing wind.

Return to the Village

 Na'im Araidi

Translated by Jay Shir

I returned to the village
where I first learned to weep
I returned to the hill
where distances are green
and no one has use for a picture
I returned to my house of stones
hewn by my grandfathers out of bedrock
I returned to myself
and that is what I wanted.

I returned to the village
having dreamed of a difficult birth
of the word *za'atar** erased from my poems
and of a birth more difficult still
of cornstalks in the deep abandoned earth—

*An aromatic mixture of wild oregano and other herbs native to
the land of Israel; used to flavor a number of Arab dishes.

for I had dreamed of the birth of love.
I returned to the village
where I had lived in my last incarnation
out of my roots sprang ten thousand vineyards
upon the good earth
until the wind arose
and blew me far away and returned me
reincarnate and penitent.

Oh, my thirty-second dream:
here were the paths that are no more
and houses grown up like the Tower of Babel
of this heavy dream of mine—
nothing can sprout from your roots!

Where are the children of poverty
ragged as fallen leaves?
Where is my village that was,
where the old paths' names
have been taken by tarmac roads?
Oh, my little village that was once,
swollen now into civilization—
I returned to the village
where the barking of dogs has died away

and the dovecote has become an electric tower.
All the peasants I would sing with,
sing haying songs in nightingale's voice,
are workers now with smoke in their throats.
Where are all those who were, who are no longer?

Oh, this heavy dream of mine—
I returned to the village
running from civilization;
came to the village
as one who goes from exile into exile.

St. Roach

 MURIEL RUKEYSER

St. Roch is the patron saint of plague victims.

*F*or that I never knew you, I only learned to dread you,
for that I never touched you, they told me you are filth,
they showed me by every action to despise your kind;
for that I saw my people making war on you,
I could not tell you apart, one from another,
for that in childhood I lived in places clear of you,
for that all the people I knew met you by
crushing you, stamping you to death, they poured
　　boiling water on you, they flushed you down,
for that I could not tell one from another
only that you were dark, fast on your feet, and slender.
　　Not like me.
For that I did not know your poems
And that I do not know any of your sayings
And that I cannot speak or read your language
And that I do not sing your songs

And that I do not teach our children
           to eat your food
           or know your poems
           or sing your songs
But that we say you are filthing our food
But that we know you not at all.

Yesterday I looked at one of you for the first time.
You were lighter than the others in color, that was
      neither good nor bad.
I was really looking for the first time.
You seemed troubled and witty.

Today I touched one of you for the first time.
You were startled, you ran, you fled away
Fast as a dancer, light, strange and lovely to the touch.
I reach, I touch, I begin to know you.

America

 CLAUDE McKAY

*A*lthough she feeds me bread of bitterness,
And sinks into my throat her tiger's tooth,
Stealing my breath of life, I will confess
I love this cultured hell that tests my youth!
Her vigor flows like tides into my blood,
Giving me strength erect against her hate.
Her bigness sweeps my being like a flood.
Yet as a rebel fronts a king in state,
I stand within her walls with not a shred
Of terror, malice, not a word of jeer.
Darkly I gaze into the days ahead,
And see her might and granite wonders there,
Beneath the touch of Time's unerring hand,
Like priceless treasures sinking in the sand.

The Sleep Writer

 MAGGIE ANDERSON

*L*ovely afternoon. The firing squad.
Bottles lined up in the sun.
Dahlias. Men in uniform. Daffodils.
Children with satchels coming home from school.
I am writing in my sleep. The journey here
was not very long, only a little cold,
the fast horses of exhaustion pulled me.
Too many people, I write, *are watching*
what we do. Too much sun on the green glass.
The firing squad. The lovely afternoon.

Passengers

 BILLY COLLINS

*A*t the gate, I sit in a row of blue seats
with the possible company of my death,
this sprawling miscellany of people—
carry-on bags and paperbacks—

that could be gathered in a flash
into a band of pilgrims on the last open road.
Not that I think
if our plane crumpled into a mountain

we would all ascend together,
holding hands like a ring of skydivers,
into a sudden gasp of brightness,
or that there would be some common place

for us to reunite to jubilize the moment,
some spaceless, pillarless Greece
where we could, at the count of three,
toss our ashes into the sunny air.

It's just that the way that man has his
    briefcase
so carefully arranged,
the way that girl is cooling her tea,
and the flow of the comb that woman

passes through her daughter's hair . . .
and when you consider the altitude,
the secret parts of the engines,
and all the hard water and the deep canyons
    below . . .

well, I just think it would be good if one of us
maybe stood up and said a few words,
or, so as not to involve the police,
at least quietly wrote something down.

After the Shipwreck

 Alicia Ostriker

*L*ost, drifting, on the current, as the sun pours down
Like syrup, drifting into afternoon,

The raft endlessly rocks, tips, and we say to each other:
Here is where we will store the rope, the dried meat,
    the knife,

The medical kit, the biscuits, and the cup.
We will divide the water fairly and honestly.

Black flecks in the air produce dizziness.
Somebody raises a voice and says: Listen, we know
    there is land

Somewhere, in some direction. We must know it.
And there is the landfall, cerulean mountain-range

On the horizon: there in our minds. Then nothing
But the beauty of ocean,

Numberless waves like living, hysterical heads,
The sun increasingly magnificent,

A sunset wind hitting us. As the spray begins
To coat us with salt, we stop talking. We try to
    remember.

What I Believe

 Michael Blumenthal

I believe there is no justice,
but that cottongrass and bunchberry
grow on the mountain.

I believe that a scorpion's sting
will kill a man,
but that his wife will remarry.

I believe that, the older we get,
the weaker the body,
but the stronger the soul.

I believe that if you roll over at night
in an empty bed,
the air consoles you.

I believe that no one is spared
the darkness,
and no one gets all of it.

I believe we all drown eventually
in a sea of our making,
but that the land belongs to someone else.

I believe in destiny.
And I believe in free will.

I believe that, when all
the clocks break,
time goes on without them.

And I believe that whatever
pulls us under,
will do so gently,

so as not to disturb anyone,
so as not to interfere
with what we believe in.

To Those Born Later (PART 1)

BERTOLT BRECHT

Translated by John Willett et al.

Truly, I live in dark times!
The guileless word is folly. A smooth forehead
Suggests insensitivity. The man who laughs
Has simply not yet had
The terrible news.

What kind of times are they, when
A talk about trees is almost a crime
Because it implies silence about so many horrors?
That man there calmly crossing the street
Is already perhaps beyond the reach of his friends
Who are in need?

It is true I still earn my keep
But, believe me, that is only an accident.
Nothing I do gives me the right to eat my fill.
By chance I've been spared. (If my luck breaks,
    I am lost.)

They say to me: Eat and drink! Be glad you have it!
But how can I eat and drink if I snatch what I eat
From the starving, and
My glass of water belongs to one dying of thirst?
And yet I eat and drink.

I would also like to be wise.
In the old books it says what wisdom is:
To shun the strife of the world and to live out
Your brief time without fear
Also to get along without violence
To return good for evil
Not to fulfil your desires but to forget them
Is accounted wise.
All this I cannot do:
Truly, I live in dark times.

III

TRY *to* PRAISE *the* MUTILATED WORLD

Affirmations and Rejoicings

The Peace of Wild Things

 WENDELL BERRY

When despair for the world grows in me
and I wake in the night at the least sound
in fear of what my life and my children's lives may be,
I go and lie down where the wood drake
rests in his beauty on the water, and the great heron
    feeds.
I come into the peace of wild things
who do not tax their lives with forethought
of grief. I come into the presence of still water.
And I feel above me the day-blind stars
waiting with their light. For a time
I rest in the grace of the world, and am free.

Northern Pike

 James Wright

All right. Try this,
Then. Every body
I know and care for,
And every body
Else is going
To die in a loneliness
I can't imagine and a pain
I don't know. We had
To go on living. We
Untangled the net, we slit
The body of this fish
Open from the hinge of the tail
To a place beneath the chin
I wish I could sing of.
I would just as soon we let
The living go on living.
An old poet whom we believe in
Said the same thing, and so
We paused among the dark cattails and prayed

For the muskrats,
For the ripples below their tails,
For the little movements that we knew the crawdads
    were making under water,
For the right-hand wrist of my cousin who is a
    policeman.
We prayed for the game warden's blindness.
We prayed for the road home.
We ate the fish.

There must be something very beautiful in my body,
I am so happy.

Try to Praise
the Mutilated World

 Adam Zagajewski

Translated by Clare Cavanagh

Try to praise the mutilated world.
Remember June's long days,
and wild strawberries, drops of wine, the dew.
The nettles that methodically overgrow
the abandoned homesteads of exiles.
You must praise the mutilated world.
You watched the stylish yachts and ships;
one of them had a long trip ahead of it,
while salty oblivion awaited others.
You've seen the refugees heading nowhere,
you've heard the executioners sing joyfully.
You should praise the mutilated world.
Remember the moments when we were together
in a white room and the curtain fluttered.
Return in thought to the concert where music flared.
You gathered acorns in the park in autumn

and leaves eddied over the earth's scars.
Praise the mutilated world
and the gray feather a thrush lost,
and the gentle light that strays and vanishes
and returns.

So Much Happiness

 NAOMI SHIHAB NYE

*I*t is difficult to know what to do with so much happiness.
With sadness there is something to rub against,
a wound to tend with lotion and cloth.
When the world falls in around you, you have pieces to
    pick up,
something to hold in your hands, like ticket stubs
    or change.

But happiness floats.
It doesn't need you to hold it down.
It doesn't need anything.
Happiness lands on the roof of the next house, singing,
and disappears when it wants to.
You are happy either way.
Even the fact that you once lived in a peaceful tree house
and now live over a quarry of noise and dust
cannot make you unhappy.
Everything has a life of its own,
it too could wake up filled with possibilities

of coffee cake and ripe peaches,
and love even the floor which needs to be swept,
the soiled linens and scratched records. . . .

Since there is no place large enough
to contain so much happiness,
you shrug, you raise your hands, and it flows out of you
into everything you touch. You are not responsible.
You take no credit, as the night sky takes no credit
for the moon, but continues to hold it, and share it,
and in that way, be known.

You Must Sing

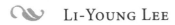 Li-Young Lee

*H*e sings in his father's arms, sings his father
to sleep, all the while seeing how on that face
grown suddenly strange, wasting to shadow,
time moves. Stern time. Sweet time. Because his father

asked, he sings; because they are wholly lost.
How else, in immaculate noon, will each find
each, who are so close now? So close and lost.
His voice stands at windows, runs everywhere.

Was death giant? O, how will he find his
father? They are so close. Was death a guest?
By which door did it come? All the day's doors
are closed. He must go out of those hours, that house,

the enfolding limbs, go burdened to learn:
you must sing to be found; when found, you must sing.

Things to Think

 ROBERT BLY

Think in ways you've never thought before
If the phone rings, think of it as carrying a message
Larger than anything you've ever heard,
Vaster than a hundred lines of Yeats.

Think that someone may bring a bear to your door,
Maybe wounded and deranged; or think that a moose
Has risen out of the lake, and he's carrying on his antlers
A child of your own whom you've never seen.

When someone knocks on the door, think that he's about
To give you something large: tell you you're forgiven,
Or that it's not necessary to work all the time, or that it's
Been decided that if you lie down no one will die.

Courage

 ANNE SEXTON

*I*t is in the small things we see it.
The child's first step,
as awesome as an earthquake.
The first time you rode a bike,
wallowing up the sidewalk.
The first spanking when your heart
went on a journey all alone.
When they called you crybaby
or poor or fatty or crazy
and made you into an alien,
you drank their acid
and concealed it.

Later,
if you faced the death of bombs and bullets
you did not do it with a banner,
you did it with only a hat to
cover your heart.
You did not fondle the weakness inside you

though it was there.
Your courage was a small coal
that you kept swallowing.
If your buddy saved you
and died himself in so doing,
then his courage was not courage,
it was love; love as simple as shaving soap.

Later,
if you have endured a great despair,
then you did it alone,
getting a transfusion from the fire,
picking the scabs off your heart,
then wringing it out like a sock.
Next, my kinsman, you powdered your sorrow,
you gave it a back rub
and then you covered it with a blanket
and after it had slept a while
it woke to the wings of the roses
and was transformed.

Later,
when you face old age and its natural conclusion
your courage will still be shown in the little ways,

each spring will be a sword you'll sharpen,
those you love will live in a fever of love,
and you'll bargain with the calendar
and at the last moment
when death opens the back door
you'll put on your carpet slippers
and stride out.

Throw Yourself Like Seed

 MIGUEL DE UNAMUNO

Translated by Robert Bly

Shake off this sadness, and recover your spirit;
sluggish you will never see the wheel of fate
that brushes your heel as it turns going by,
the man who wants to live is the man in whom life
    is abundant.

Now you are only giving food to that final pain
which is slowly winding you in the nets of death,
but to live is to work, and the only thing
    which lasts
is the work; start then, turn to the work.

Throw yourself like seed as you walk, and into your
    own field,
don't turn your face for that would be to turn it
    to death,
and do not let the past weigh down your motion.

Leave what's alive in the furrow, what's dead
     in yourself,
for life does not move in the same way as a group
     of clouds;
from your work you will be able one day to
     gather yourself.

Somehow we survive

 DENNIS BRUTUS

Somehow we survive
and tenderness, frustrated, does not wither.

Investigating searchlights rake
our naked unprotected contours;

over our heads the monolithic decalogue
of fascist prohibition glowers
and teeters for a catastrophic fall;

boots club the peeling door.

But somehow we survive
severance, deprivation, loss

Patrols uncoil along the asphalt dark
hissing their menace to our lives,

most cruel, all our land is scarred with terror,
rendered unlovely and unlovable;
sundered are we and all our passionate surrender

but somehow tenderness survives.

May 1915

   CHARLOTTE MEW

*L*et us remember Spring will come again
To the scorched, blackened woods, where the
    wounded trees
Wait, with their old wise patience for the
    heavenly rain,
Sure of the sky: sure of the sea to send its healing breeze,
    Sure of the sun. And even as to these
        Surely the Spring, when God shall please,
    Will come again like a divine surprise
To those who sit today with their great Dead, hands in
    their hands, eyes in their eyes,
At one with love, at one with Grief: blind to the scattered
    things and changing skies.

IV

WE ARE RUNNING

*Warnings
and Instructions*

we are running

 LUCILLE CLIFTON

*W*e are running
running and
time is clocking us
from the edge like an only
daughter.
our mothers stream before us,
cradling their breasts in their
hands.
oh pray that what we want
is worth this running,
pray that what we're running
toward
is what we want.

Leap Before You Look

 W. H. AUDEN

*T*he sense of danger must not disappear:
The way is certainly both short and steep,
However gradual it looks from here;
Look if you like, but you will have to leap.

Tough-minded men get mushy in their sleep
And break the by-laws any fool can keep;
It is not the convention but the fear
That has a tendency to disappear.

The worried efforts of the busy heap,
The dirt, the imprecision, and the beer
Produce a few smart wisecracks every year;
Laugh if you can, but you will have to leap.

The clothes that are considered right to wear
Will not be either sensible or cheap,
So long as we consent to live like sheep
And never mention those who disappear.

Much can be said for social savoir-fairs,
But to rejoice when no one else is there
Is even harder than it is to weep;
No one is watching, but you have to leap.

A solitude ten thousand fathoms deep
Sustains the bed on which we lie, my dear:
Although I love you, you will have to leap;
Our dream of safety has to disappear.

December 1940

FROM *The Cure at Troy*

 SEAMUS HEANEY

*H*uman beings suffer,
They torture one another,
They get hurt and get hard.
No poem or play or song
Can fully right a wrong
Inflicted and endured.

The innocent in gaols
Beat on their bars together.
A hunger-striker's father
Stands in the graveyard dumb.
The police widow in veils
Faints at the funeral home.

History says, Don't hope
On this side of the grave.
But then, once in a lifetime
The longed-for tidal wave
Of justice can rise up,
And hope and history rhyme.

So hope for a great sea-change
On the far side of revenge.
Believe that a further shore
Is reachable from here.
Believe in miracles
And cures and healing wells.

Call miracle self-healing:
The utter, self-revealing
Double-take of feeling.
If there's fire on the mountain
Or lightning and storm
And a god speaks from the sky

That means someone is hearing
The outcry and the birth-cry
Of new life at its term.
It means once in a lifetime
That justice can rise up
And hope and history rhyme.

I know the truth—
give up all other truths!

 ## MARINA TSVETAYEVA

Translated by Elaine Feinstein

I know the truth—give up all other truths!
No need for people anywhere on earth to struggle.
Look—it is evening, look, it is nearly night:
what do you speak of, poets, lovers, generals?

The wind is level now, the earth is wet with dew,
the storm of stars in the sky will turn to quiet.
And soon all of us will sleep under the earth, we
who never let each other sleep above it.

Shemà

 PRIMO LEVI

*Translated by Ruth Feldman
and Brian Swann*

You who live secure
In your warm houses,
Who return at evening to find
Hot food and friendly faces:

 Consider whether this is a man,
 Who labours in the mud
 Who knows no peace
 Who fights for a crust of bread
 Who dies at a yes or a no.
 Consider whether this is a woman,
 Without hair or name
 With no more strength to remember
 Eyes empty and womb cold
 As a frog in winter.

Consider that this has been:
I commend these words to you.
Engrave them on your hearts
When you are in your house, when you
    walk on your way,
When you go to bed, when you rise.
Repeat them to your children.
Or may your house crumble,
Disease render you powerless,
Your offspring avert their faces from you.

An Earthly Beauty

 JANE HIRSHFIELD

*O*thers have described
the metal bull placed over fire,
it singing while the man inside it died.
Which emperor listened, in which country,
doesn't matter, though surely
the thing itself was built by slaves.
An unearthly music, all reports agree.
We—the civilized—hearing this story,
recoil from it in horror: Not us. Not ours.
But why does my heart look back at me,
reproachful? Why does the bull?

You Will Forget

 CHENJERAI HOVE

*I*f you stay in comfort too long
you will not know
the weight of a water pot
on the bald head of the village woman

You will forget
the weight of three bundles of thatch grass
on the sinewy neck of the woman
whose baby cries on her back
for a blade of grass in its eyes

Sure, if you stay in comfort too long
you will not know the pain
of child birth without a nurse in white

You will forget
the thirst, the cracked dusty lips
of the woman in the valley
on her way to the headman who isn't there

You will forget
the pouring pain of a thorn prick
with a load on the head.
If you stay in comfort too long

You will forget
the wailing in the valley
of women losing a husband in the mines.

You will forget
the rough handshake of coarse palms
full of teary sorrow at the funeral.

If you stay in comfort too long
You will not hear
the shrieky voice of old warriors sing
the songs of fresh stored battlefields.

You will forget
the unfeeling bare feet
gripping the warm soil turned by the plough

You will forget
the voice of the season talking to the oxen.

The City

 C. P. Cavafy

Translated by Rae Dalven

You said, "I will go to another land, I will go to
    another sea.
Another city will be found, a better one than this.
Every effort of mine is a condemnation of fate;
and my heart is—like a corpse—buried.
How long will my mind remain in this wasteland.
Wherever I turn my eyes, wherever I may look
I see black ruins of my life here,
where I spent so many years destroying and wasting."

You will find no new lands, you will find no
    other seas.
The city will follow you. You will roam the same
streets. And you will age in the same neighbourhoods;
and you will grow gray in these same houses.
Always you will arrive in this city. Do not hope for
    any other—

There is no ship for you, there is no road.
As you have destroyed your life here
in this little corner, you have ruined it in the
    entire world.

The Summer-Camp Bus Pulls Away from the Curb

 SHARON OLDS

Whatever he needs, he has or doesn't
have by now.
Whatever the world is going to do to him
it has started to do. With a pencil and two
Hardy Boys and a peanut butter sandwich and
grapes he is on his way, there is nothing
more we can do for him. Whatever is
stored in his heart, he can use, now.
Whatever he has laid up in his mind
he can call on. What he does not have
he can lack. The bus gets smaller and smaller, as one
folds a flag at the end of a ceremony,
onto itself, and onto itself, until
only a heavy wedge remains.
Whatever his exuberant soul
can do for him, it is doing right now.
Whatever his arrogance can do

it is doing to him. Everything
that's been done to him, he will now do.
Everything that's been placed in him
will come out, now, the contents of a trunk
unpacked and lined up on a bunk in the underpine
    light.

Speech to the Young. Speech to the Progress-Toward.

 GWENDOLYN BROOKS

Say to them,
say to the down-keepers,
the sun-slappers,
the self-soilers,
the harmony-hushers,

"Even if you are not ready for day
it cannot always be night."
You will be right.
For that is the hard home-run.

And remember:
live not for Battles Won.
Live not for The-End-of-the-Song.
Live in the along.

V

END *and* BEGINNING

War and Rumors of War

A Soldier—His Prayer

 Anonymous

*This anonymous poem was blown
into a slit trench in Tunisia during a
heavy bombardment in the early days
of World War II.*

Stay with me, God. The night is dark,
The night is cold: my little spark
Of courage dies. The night is long;
Be with me, God, and make me strong.

I love a game; I love a fight.
I hate the dark; I love the light.
I love my child; I love my wife.
I am no coward. I love Life,

Life with its change of mood and shade.
I want to live. I'm not afraid,
But me and mine are hard to part;
Oh, unknown God, lift up my heart.

You stilled the waters at Dunkirk
And saved Your Servants. All Your work
Is wonderful, dear God. You strode
Before us down that dreadful road.

We were alone, and hope had fled;
We loved our country and our dead,
And could not shame them; so we stayed
The course, and were not much afraid.

Dear God that nightmare road! And then
That sea! We got there—we were men.
My eyes were blind, my feet were torn,
My soul sang like a bird at dawn!

I knew that death is but a door.
I knew what we were fighting for:
Peace for the kids, our brothers freed,
A kinder world, a cleaner breed.

I'm but the son my mother bore,
A simple man, and nothing more.
But—God of strength and gentleness,
Be pleased to make me nothing less.

Help me, O God, when Death is near
To mock the haggard face of fear,
That when I fall—if fall I must—
My soul may triumph in the Dust.

A whole night

 GIUSEPPI UNGARETTI

Translated by Ivo Mosley

A whole night,
Thrown down near a friend
Already butchered
With his mouth
Baring its teeth
Toward the full moon:
With the congestion
Of his hands
Penetrating my silence,
I've written letters
Full of love.

Never have I been
So
Attached to life.

Base Details

 Siegfried Sassoon

If I were fierce and bald and short of breath,
   I'd live with scarlet Majors at the Base,
And speed glum heroes up the line to death.
   You'd see me with my puffy petulant face,
Guzzling and gulping in the best hotel,
   Reading the Roll of Honor. "Poor young chap,"
I'd say—"I used to know his father well.
   Yes, we've lost heavily in this last scrap."
And when the war is done and youth stone dead,
I'd toddle safely home and die—in bed.

The Inner Part

 Louis Simpson

When they had won the war
And for the first time in history
Americans were the most important people—

When the leading citizens no longer lived in
    their shirt sleeves,
And their wives did not scratch in public;
Just when they'd stopped saying "Gosh!"—

When their daughters seemed as sensitive
As the tip of a fly rod,
And their sons were as smooth as a V-8 engine—

Priests, examining the entrails of birds,
Found the heart misplaced, and seeds
As black as death, emitting a strange odor.

How to Kill

 KEITH DOUGLAS

*U*nder the parabola of a ball,
a child turning into a man,
I looked into the air too long.
The ball fell into my hand, it sang
in the closed fist: *Open Open*
Behold a gift designed to kill.

Now in my dial of glass appears
the soldier who is going to die.
He smiles, and moves about in ways
his mother knows, habits of his.
The wires touch his face; I cry
NOW. Death, like a familiar, hears

and look, has made a man of dust
of a man of flesh. This sorcery
I do. Being damned, I am amused
to see the center of love diffused
and the waves of love travel into vacancy.
How easy it is to make a ghost.

The weightless mosquito touches
her tiny shadow on the stone,
and with how like, how infinite
a lightness, man and shadow meet.
They fuse. A shadow is a man
When the mosquito death approaches.

The Casualties

 J. P. CLARK-BEKEDEREMO

To Chinua Achebe

The casualties are not only those who are dead;
They are well out of it.
The casualties are not only those who are wounded,
Though they await burial by instalment.
The casualties are not only those who have lost
Persons or property, hard as it is
To grope for a touch that some
May not know is not there.
The casualties are not only those led away by night;
The cell is a cruel place, sometimes a haven,
Nowhere as absolute as the grave.
The casualties are not only those who started
A fire and now cannot put it out. Thousands
Are burning that had no say in the matter.
The casualties are not only those who escaping

The shattered shell become prisoners in
A fortress of falling walls.

The casualties are many, and a good number well
Outside the scenes of ravage and wreck;
They are the emissaries of rift,
So smug in smoke-rooms they haunt abroad,
They do not see the funeral piles
At home eating up the forests.
They are the wandering minstrels who, beating on
The drums of the human heart, draw the world
Into a dance with rites it does not know
The drums overwhelm the guns . . .
Caught in the clash of counter claims and charges
When not in the niche others have left,
We fall,
All casualties of the war,
Because we cannot hear each other speak,
Because eyes have ceased to see the face from the
    crowd,
Because whether we know or
Do not know the extent of wrong on all sides,
We are characters now other than before
The war began, the stay-at-home unsettled

By taxes and rumours, the looters for office
And wares, fearful every day the owners may return,
We are all casualties,
All sagging as are
The cases celebrated for kwashiorkor,
The unforeseen camp-follower of not just our war.

Facing It

 YUSEF KOMUNYAKAA

*M*y black face fades,
hiding inside the black granite.
I said I wouldn't,
dammit: No tears.
I'm stone. I'm flesh.
My clouded reflection eyes me
like a bird of prey, the profile of night
slanted against morning. I turn
this way—the stone lets me go.
I turn that way—I'm inside
the Vietnam Veterans Memorial
again, depending on the light
to make a difference.
I go down the 58,022 names,
half-expecting to find
my own in letters like smoke.
I touch the name Andrew Johnson;
I see the booby trap's white flash.
Names shimmer on a woman's blouse

but when she walks away
the names stay on the wall.
Brushstrokes flash, a red bird's
wings cutting across my stare.
The sky. A plane in the sky.
A white vet's image floats
closer to me, then his pale eyes
look through mine. I'm a window.
He's lost his right arm
inside the stone. In the black mirror
a woman's trying to erase names:
No, she's brushing a boy's hair.

The Conscientious Objector

 KARL SHAPIRO

The gates clanged and they walked you into jail
More tense than felons but relieved to find
The hostile world shut out, the flags that dripped
From every mother's windowpane, obscene
The bloodlust sweating from the public heart,
The dog authority slavering at your throat.
A sense of quiet, of pulling down the blind
Possessed you. Punishment you felt was clean.

The decks, the catwalks, and the narrow light
Composed a ship. This was a mutinous crew
Troubling the captains for plain decencies,
A Mayflower brim with pilgrims headed out
To establish new theocracies to west,
A Noah's ark coasting the topmost seas
Ten miles above the sodomites and fish.
These inmates loved the only living doves.

Like all men hunted from the world you made
A good community, voyaging the storm

To no safe Plymouth or green Ararat;
Trouble or calm, the men with Bibles prayed,
The gaunt politicals construed our hate.
The opposite of all armies, you were best
Opposing uniformity and yourselves;
Prison and personality were your fate.

You suffered not so physically but knew
Maltreatment, hunger, ennui of the mind.
Well might the soldier kissing the hot beach
Erupting in his face damn all your kind.
Yet you who saved neither yourselves nor us
Are equally with those who shed the blood
The heroes of our cause. Your conscience is
What we come back to in the armistice.

End and Beginning

 WISLAWA SZYMBORSKA

Translated by Joseph Brodsky

*A*fter each war
somebody has to clear up
put things in order
by itself it won't happen.

Somebody's got to push
rubble to the highway shoulder
making way
for the carts filled up with corpses.

Someone might trudge
through muck and ashes,
sofa springs,
splintered glass
and blood-soaked rugs.

Somebody has to haul
beams for propping a wall,

another put glass in a window
and hang the door on hinges.

This is not photogenic
and takes years.
All the cameras have left already
for another war.

Bridges are needed
also new railroad stations.
Tatters turn into sleeves
for rolling up.

Somebody, broom in hand,
still recalls how it was.
Someone whose head was not
torn away listens nodding.
But nearby already
begin to bustle those
who'll need persuasion.

Somebody still at times
digs up from under the bushes

some rusty quibble
to add to burning refuse.

Those who knew
what this was all about
must yield to those
who know little
or less than little
essentially nothing.

In the grass that has covered
effects in causes
somebody must recline,
a stalk of rye in the teeth,
ogling the clouds.

Politics

 WILLIAM BUTLER YEATS

In our time the destiny of man
presents its meaning in political terms.
—Thomas Mann

*H*ow can I, that girl standing there,
My attention fix
On Roman or on Russian
Or on Spanish politics?
Yet here's a travelled man that knows
What he talks about,
And there's a politician
That has read and thought,
And maybe what they say is true
Of war and war's alarms,
But O that I were young again
And held her in my arms!

1939

VI
LITTLE PRAYERS
Meditations and Conversations

Town of Finding Out
About the Love of God

 ANNE CARSON

I had made a mistake.
Before this day.
Now my suitcase is ready.
Two hardboiled eggs.
For the journey are stored.
In the places where.
My eyes were.
How could it be otherwise?
Like a current.
Carrying a twig.
The sobbing made me.
Audible to you.

Little Prayers

 PAUL GOODMAN

1.

Creator Spirit, who dost lightly hover
whence I know not, and why to me I never
    questioned, come. Do visit thy lover
    after Thy long absence. I turn over

awaking in the morning: Thou art not
there to my touch nor is a substitute
    there, but nothing nothing at all to talk
    to and make love when I awake.

2.

O spirit wise, somewhere shine!
so I can squander me again.
    I ask it, if ever I tried hard
    to eke me out a livelihood

from my grudging city, and if ever
I have been patient to preserve

opportunity my sweet
muse, my darling, my flirt.

3.

The tons of trucks that thunder by
perturb not me who thread my way.
    The sun is roaring through the smoke
    by grace on me who stand and look.

I do not know if happiness
will show before me like a face
    or rise within me like a song,
    deliberately I move along.

4.

The flashing shadow of the sun
in the bloody window made me turn
    and face his face, and I saw
    over his shoulder You.

Everywhere I look about
are there outlines of truth and art
    breeding in the dark of this
    moment at the edge of the abyss.

5.

Novices of art
understate
    what has them by the throat
    the climax; You speak out

for me, spirit who affright
me in the lonely night,
    nor do I know till I express it
    the message boiling in my breast.

Psalm 5

 ERNESTO CARDENAL

Translated by Robert Márquez

Give ear to my words, O Lord,
                              Harken unto my moaning
Pay heed to my protest
For you are not a God friendly to dictators
neither are you a partisan of their politics
nor are you influenced by their propaganda
neither are you in league with the gangster

There is no sincerity in their speeches
nor in their press releases

They speak of peace in their speeches
while they increase their war production
They speak of peace at Peace Conferences
and secretly prepare for war
                              Their lying radios roar into the night
their desks are strewn with criminal intentions
But you will deliver me from their plans

They speak through the mouth of the submachine gun
Their flashing tongues are bayonets . . .

Punish them, O Lord
                       Thwart them in their policies
confuse their memorandums
                              obstruct their programs

At the hour of Alarm
you shall be with me
you shall be my refuge on the day of the Bomb

To him who believes not in the lies of their commercial
                                         messages
nor in their publicity campaigns nor in their political
campaigns
                              you will give your blessing.
With love do you compass him
                   as with armor-plated tanks.

On Prayer

 Czeslaw Milosz

Translated by Robert Hass

You ask me how to pray to someone who is not.
All I know is that prayer constructs a velvet bridge
And walking it we are aloft, as on a springboard,
Above landscapes the color of ripe gold
Transformed by a magic stopping of the sun.
That bridge leads to the shore of Reversal
Where everything is just the opposite and the word *is*
Unveils a meaning we hardly envisioned.
Notice: I say *we;* there, every one, separately,
Feels compassion for others entangled in the flesh
And knows that if there is no other shore
They will walk that aerial bridge all the same.

Crucifixion

  HAYDEN CARRUTH

You understand the colors on the hillside have faded,
   we have the gray and brown and lavender of
      late autumn,
the apple and pear trees have lost their leaves, the mist
   of November is often with us, especially in
      the afternoon
and toward evening, as it was today when I sat gazing
   up into the orchard for a long time the way I do now,
thinking of how I died last winter and was revived.
   And I tell you I saw there a cross with a man nailed
to it, silvery in the mist, and I said to him: "Are you
   the Christ?" And he must have heard me, for in his
agony, twisted as he was, he nodded his head affirmatively,
   up and down, once and twice. And a little way off
I saw another cross with another man nailed to it,
   twisting and nodding, and then another and another,
ranks and divisions of crosses straggling like exhausted
   legions upward among the misty trees, each cross
with a silvery, writhing, twisting, nodding, naked

figure nailed to it, and some of them were women.
The hill was filled with crucifixion. Should I not be
    telling you this? Is it excessive? But I know something
about death now, I know how silent it is, silent, even
    when the pain is shrieking and screaming. And tonight
is very silent and very dark. When I looked I saw
    nothing out there, only my own reflected head nodding
a little in the window glass. It was as if the Christ
    had nodded to me, all those writhing silvery images
on the hillside, and after a while I nodded back to him.

Souls

 DANNIE ABSE

"After the last breath, eyelids must be closed
quickly. For eyes are windows of the soul
—that shy thing which is immortal. And none
should see its exit vulnerably exposed,"

proclaimed the bearded man on Yom Kippur.
Grownups believed in the soul. Otherwise
why did grandfather murmur the morning prayer,
"Lord, the soul Thou hast given me is pure"?

Near the kitchen door where they notched my height
a mirror hung. There I saw the big eyes
of a boy. I could not picture the soul
immaterial and immortal. A cone of light?

Those two black zeros the soul's windows? Daft!
Later, at medical school, I learnt of
the pineal gland, its size a cherrystone,
vestige of the third eye, and laughed.

But seven colors hide in light's disguise
and the blue sky's black. No wonder Egyptians
once believed, in their metamorphosis,
souls soared, became visible: butterflies.

Now old, I'm credulous. Superstition clings.
After the melting eyes and devastation
of Hiroshima, they say butterflies, crazed,
flew about, fluttering soundless things.

Concerning That Prayer
I Cannot Make

 JANE MEAD

*J*esus, I am cruelly lonely
and I do not know what I have done
nor do I suspect that you will answer me.

And, what is more, I have spent
these bare months bargaining
with my soul as if I could make her
promise to love me when now it seems
that what I meant when I said "soul"
was that the river reflects
the railway bridge just as the sky
says it should—it speaks *that* language.

I do not know who you are.

I come here every day
to be beneath this bridge,
to sit beside this river,

so I *must* have seen the way
the clouds just slide
under the rusty arch—
without snagging on the bolts,
how they are borne along on the dark water—
I must have noticed their fluent speed
and also how that tattered blue T-shirt
remains snagged on the crown
of the mostly sunk dead tree
despite the current's constant pulling.
Yes, somewhere in my mind there must
be the image of a sky blue T-shirt, caught,
and the white islands of ice flying by
and the light clouds flying slowly
under the bridge, though today the river's
fully melted. I must have seen.

But I did not see.

I am not equal to my longing.
Somewhere there should be a place
the exact shape of my emptiness—
there should be a place
responsible for taking one back.

The river, of course, has no mercy—
it just lifts the dead fish
toward the sea.

Of course, of course.

What I *meant* when I said "soul"
was that there should be a place.

On the far bank the warehouse lights
blink red, then green, and all the yellow
machines with their rusted scoops and lifts
sit under a thin layer of sunny frost.

And look—
my own palm—
there, slowly rocking.
It is *my* pale palm—
palm where a black pebble
is turning and turning.

Listen—
all you bare trees
burrs
brambles

pile of twigs
red and green lights flashing
muddy bottle shards
shoe half buried—listen

listen, I am holy.

Six Apologies, Lord

 OLENA KALYTIAK DAVIS

I Have Loved My Horrible Self, Lord.
I Rose, Lord, And I Rose, Lord, And I,
Dropt. Your Requirements, Lord. 'Spite Your
    Requirements, Lord,
I Have Loved The Low Voltage Of The Moon, Lord,
Until There Was No Moon Intensity Left, Lord, No
    Moon Intensity Left
For You, Lord. I Have Loved The Frivolous, The
    Fleeting, The Frightful
Clouds. Lord, I Have Loved Clouds! Do Not Forgive
    Me, Do Not
Forgive Me LordandLover, HarborandMaster,
    GuardianandBread, Do Not.
Hold Me, Lord, O, Hold Me

Accountable, Lord. I Am
Accountable. Lord.

Lord It Over Me,
Lord It Over Me, Lord. Feed Me

Hope, Lord. Feed Me
Hope, Lord, Or Break My Teeth.

Brake My Teeth, Sir,
In This My Mouth.

Eleven Addresses to the Lord (PART 1)

 JOHN BERRYMAN

*M*aster of beauty, craftsman of the snowflake,
inimitable contriver,
endower of Earth so gorgeous & different from
   the boring Moon,
thank you for such as it is my gift.

I have made up a morning prayer to you
containing with precision everything that most
   matters.
'According to Thy will' the thing begins.
It took me off & on two days. It does not aim
   at eloquence.

You have come to my rescue again & again
in my impassable, sometimes despairing years.
You have allowed my brilliant friends to
   destroy themselves
and I am still here, severely damaged, but
   functioning.

Unknowable, as I am unknown to my guinea pigs:
how can I 'love' you?
I only as far as gratitude & awe
confidently & absolutely go.

I have no idea whether we live again.
It doesn't seem likely
from either the scientific or the philosophical point
	of view
but certainly all things are possible to you,

and I believe as fixedly in the Resurrection-
	appearances to Peter and to Paul
	as I believe I sit in this blue chair.
Only that may have been a special case
to establish their initiatory faith.

Whatever your end may be, accept my amazement.
May I stand until death forever at attention
for any your least instruction or enlightenment.
I even feel sure you will assist me again, Master of
	insight & beauty.

Pax

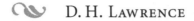 D. H. LAWRENCE

*A*ll that matters is to be at one with the living God
to be a creature in the house of the God of Life.

Like a cat asleep on a chair
at peace, in peace
and at one with the master of the house, with the mistress,
at home, at home in the house of the living,
sleeping on the hearth, and yawning before the fire.

Sleeping on the hearth of the living world
yawning at home before the fire of life
feeling the presence of the living God
like a great assurance
a deep calm in the heart
a presence
as of the master sitting at the board
in his own and greater being
in the house of life.

CREDITS

ABOUT THE EDITOR

Joan Murray is a National Poetry Series winner and the author of three books: *Queen of the Mist, Looking for the Parade,* and *The Same Water.* General editor of *The Best of Pushcart Poetry* (forthcoming) and poetry editor of the twenty-fifth-anniversary *Pushcart Prize,* she is poet-in-residence at the New York State Writers Institute.